Party An

Contents

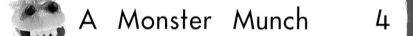

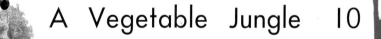

You will need:
- toothpicks
- half a melon
- fruit
- sweets
- icing
- thin slices of carrot
- a spoon

2

1. Use the icing to stick sweets on for eyes.

2. Use the spoon and the carrot to make ears.

3. Put the fruit onto the toothpicks.

4. Put the toothpicks onto the porcupine.

You will need:

- a hamburger bun
- lettuce
- cheese
- sliced meat
- olives
- tomatoes
- a toothpick

4

1. Put the sliced meat in the hamburger bun.

2. Use the cheese to make teeth.

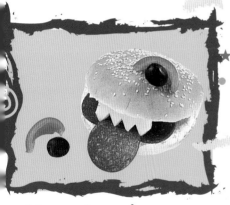

3. Use the olives and tomatoes to make eyes.

4. Put the lettuce on the bun to make hair.

A FRIENDLY FACE

You will need:

- plain biscuits
- sweets
- icing
- sprinkles

1. Use the icing to stick sweets on for eyes.

2. Use the icing to stick a sweet on for a nose.

3. Use the icing to stick a sweet on for a mouth.

4. Use the icing to stick sprinkles on for hair.

7

You will need:

- a banana
- sweets
- rolled fruit
- a toothpick
- scissors

8

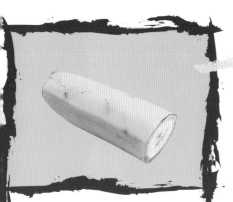

1. Cut the banana in half.

2. Pull down the peel to make wings and a tail.

3. Use the sweets for eyes and a beak. Use the toothpick to attach the beak.

4. Put the rolled fruit onto the wings, the tail, and the head.

A VEGETABLE JUNGLE

You will need:

- a carrot
- broccoli
- cauliflower
- lettuce
- olives
- toothpicks
- a knife

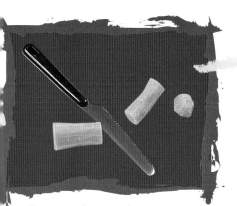

1. Cut the carrot so it is flat at the top and the bottom.

2. Use a toothpick to stick the lettuce onto the carrot.

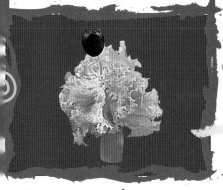

3. Put an olive on top of the toothpick.

4. Cut pieces of cauliflower and broccoli so they stand up.

A SLIMY SWAMP

You will need:

- an avocado
- a lemon
- chopped tomato
- a fork

1. Cut and peel
   the avocado.

2. Put it into a
   bowl. Squash it
   until it is smooth.

3. Add lemon juice
   so the avocado
   doesn't turn brown.

4. Add the chopped
   tomato to the
   avocado mixture.

A DELICIOUS DRINK

You will need:

- juice mix
- water
- a jug
- ice
- sliced fruit
- glasses

1. Mix the juice
with water
in the jug.

2. Add the ice.

3. Decorate the glasses
with the fruit.

15

Let's party!

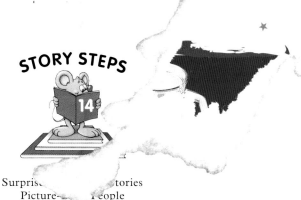

STORY STEPS

14

Surpris‿ ⸺ tories
Picture‿ ⸺ People
Party Animals
Snake's Reward
Animal Biscuits

Written by **Victoria St John**
Photographed by **Alan Gillard**
Food created by **Victoria St John**

© 2000 Shortland Publications Inc.

Published in New Zealand by
Shortland Publications,
2B Cawley Street, Ellerslie, Auckland.

Published in the United Kingdom by
Kingscourt Publishing Limited,
P.O. Box 1427, Freepost, London W6 9BR.

Published in Australia by
Shortland-Mimosa,
8 Yarra Street, Hawthorn, Victoria 3122.

05 04 03 02 01 00
10 9 8 7 6 5 4 3 2 1

Printed by Colorcraft, Hong Kong

ISBN: 0-7901-2104-2

STORY STEPS

14

Would you like
a banana bird
at your birthday party?
Find out how to make
your very own
party animals.

ISBN 0-7901-2104-2